Pushing the Limits

Also by Kenneth Lyon

A Dance Horizontal, Poems, 2023

Pushing the Limits

A Bound Collection of Boundless Poems

Kenneth Lyon

Homestead Lighthouse Press
Akron, Ohio

Pushing the Limits copyright © Kenneth Lyon 2025, Homestead Lighthouse Press, First Edition

All rights reserved. No part of this book may be reproduced or transmitted in any form without the prior written permission of the publisher.

Library of Congress Cataloging-in-Publication Data Pending

Names: Kenneth Lyon, author.

Library of Congress Control Number: 2023941518

ISBN 978-1-950475-44-5

Homestead Lighthouse Press
1314 Pontiac Ave.
Akron, OH 44307
www.homesteadlighthousepress.com

Distributed by Homestead Lighthouse Press, Daedalus Distribution, Amazon.com, Barnes & Noble

Cover & Book Design: Ray Rhamey, Ashland, OR
Cover photo by Daryl Chinn

Homestead Lighthouse Press gratefully acknowledges the generous support of its readers and patrons.

for Roberta, Sean, and Aaron

Introduction

By the Author

"Some think my right brain writes poems,
and my left balances the checkbook,
but sometimes my poems are rigid and detailed,
and my checkbook has to pay for overdrafts."

I gave my financial consultant a copy of my first published collection of poems. Knowing that I had studied electrical engineering and had an undergraduate degree in mathematics, as well as graduate degrees in creative writing, he commented that my *corpus callosum* must be busy. I had never heard that term. After looking it up in the dictionary, I thought that it would make a good book title. If the different parts of my brain tell me to think and write in certain ways, I assume my poems reflect what is going on inside my head. These thoughts must come from somewhere, and I try to push them beyond their limits. Thus, I came up with a different title for this collection, *Pushing the Limits*.

Some of these poems follow particular forms, schemes, and structures. Others appear more haphazard. As a graduate student in The Johns Hopkins University Writing Seminars, I read the American Heritage Dictionary cover to cover so that I could have all words at my disposal for poems. In this collection, you will find words that have multiples meanings, rhymes, various rhythms, and other rhetorical devices that help bring these poems to life. I enjoy writing several poems at the same time. When ideas come, I put them on paper, in my iPhone Notes, or in Word docs on my iMac. The survivors end up on my desktop, where I visit daily to revise, review, edit, or discard. Some parts of this routine are more rewarding than others. When I share my poems, I solicit feedback and make subsequent changes as my instincts dictate. My life and my poetry have a symbiotic relationship, as in the beginning of my poem "Aways Under Construction":

"I live my life
a work in progress
constant revisions..."

I read my poems out loud, and my wife often asks, "Are you talking to me?" When I write, I sometimes do not know where I am. Usually some other private place. I try to make my poems meaningful, universal, offering something for every reader to relate to. Sometimes that happens. Sometimes not. Humor also allows my readers to envision a brighter side of things that at first may appear rather sad.

As my publisher and editor Robert McDowell said, "Your manuscript is a 'day in the life' witnessing that many can and will identify with. I am impressed by the witnessing we often get here about aging and stepping into the mentor's time of life. We need more poems and art like that."

So, the choice is yours. You can look at the contents and pick a title to start, you can go from front to back, or you can just turn to any page. Put this book on a nightstand or coffee table and begin reading as you wish. Follow your curiosity and interest without limitations.

Thank you for allowing me to share these poems. I hope you find in them some meaningful imagery.

A poem is the little bird that flew into my patio glass door,
Lying dazed and bewildered on the cold concrete.
It came back to life, looked me in the eye,
Shook its wings, and flew away.

Contents

I At First Sight	1
Corpus Callosum	3
Banned	5
To Be a Poet	6
Legere, Scribere, et Recitare	11
Geoffrey and Thomas	12
57th and 7th	14
Guppies, Rasboras, Neon Tetras, and an Angel	16
In My Salad Days	17
Always Under Construction	19
My Y Chromosome Causes Chaos	20
Ambition	21
The Fortunate One	23
Special Effects	25
The Day I Didn't Get a Tattoo	27
Mon Meilleur et Mon Pire Souvenir	29
No One's Home	31
Our Lives in a Whirlpool™	32
Our Dog Wears Diapers	34
The Garden of Hedon	35
Postnuptial Agreement	37
The Succubus	38
Shopping for Sex Toys	40
Hemorrhoid Surgery Kicked My Ass	42
The Spiders on My Foot	44

Calories	46
An Everyday Occurrence	47
Witching Myself Good Luck	48

II On Second Thought — 51

October 7	53
Make Love Not War at The Pendulum, 1968	54
Educating Disturbed Children	57
Cease and Embrace	59
May Day	60
Ecstatic Discovery and Tragic Recovery	62
Chicxulub	64
In the Valley of Dead Stars	65
Bas Relief	69
We the People	70
Hold the Phone	73
When Billionaires Go Home	74
just asking	76
The Last Chapter	78
The Maven	79
Multiple Choice	84
Attack of the Mutant Ninja Similes	85
Happy as a Clam at High Tide	86

III At Peace — 89

The Extraordinary Escapades of Lilly and River	91
Skipping Stones	94
Stairs to the Ocean	96

The End of Travel	97
Lithe or Deaf	99
Everything Hurts	100
A Date with Dr. Schnaser	101
Why Not Complain	102
The Private Thoughts of Justin Time	103
Just Us and Our Stuff	104
The Great Wall at Badaling, 1983	107
Ten Days in the Holy Land, 2007	109
On the Other Side	120
Epilogue	122
Ship in a Bottle	124
Sunken Ships	126
Aphrodite	128
Waiting in ER	129
Another First Seder	131
Boulder Drop	134
In Peace Rest	136
The Last Sunday in Sacramento	137
About the Author	138
Acknowledgments	139

I

At First Sight

Corpus Callosum

My left barely communicates with my right.
It takes a lot of conscientious nerve
To move from one hemisphere to the other,
Pack all my bags and remember what I'm doing,
Wake up every morning to check the calendar,
Stay alert and coordinate my efforts.

Every day I send signals,
Try my best to cross the bridge,
Sense what's going on around me,
Get my muscles moving, invigorate my memory,
Sound like I know what I'm talking about,
And solve all recurring problems within reason.

My eyes may appear exhausted,
As my lobes do their dirty work,
Stay functional and keep up the pace,
Until I have another birthday,
Follow the instructions to bake a cake,
And blow out all the candles in one breath.

So far I don't need medication or therapy,
Just an exercise routine and nutritious meals.
Some think my right brain writes poems,
And my left balances the checkbook,
But sometimes my poems are rigid and detailed,
And my checkbook has to pay for overdrafts.

What the hell is going on inside my head,
Are some of my cells becoming dead?
Ideas and thoughts are born in vapors,
And once on paper need to be cultured,
Like reproducing bacteria alive in a petri dish,
These eccentric notions will make some sense I wish.

Banned

Put this poem on the list
Remove it from the library
Sell it on the black market
For more than it's worth
Talk about it in back alleys
Behind my back and yours
In whispers wearing sunglasses
And mouths with open jaws
Dropping and slinking around
In the middle of the night
Under the covers
Looking for the dirty parts
Trying to figure out
What's wrong with it
How it will harm children
Turn them into miscreants
Sacrilegious social deviants
Type it in boldface on headlines
Spur public protests
Make signs and banners
And raise the price
To sell at secret auctions
Just don't dispose of it
Only deride and scoff at it
As I make another deposit
And bank my profit

To Be a Poet

You have to build your house from the ground up,
Decorate with care,
Put perfume in the air,
And live your life as a poem
That someone wrote for you
That you get to rewrite and revise.

Develop a vision that can grow out of itself,
And pay attention to myriad details
That knock on your door, settle on the floor
To keep you on your toes as you compose
For the key you're playing and every chord,
OMG major, no longer A minor,
Or you'll get an F sharp diminished.
Count the days on the calendar,
The leap years to synchronize with the solar system,
The rules in the latest driver's manual
So you can get poetic license,
How old you are so you can vote,
Buy alcohol and tell the truth.

You should be aware of your space,
Balance your checkbook to the penny,
Use a digital thermometer when you cook,
Measure the four seasonings
Parsley, sage, rosemary, and thyme,
Keep track of time every second,

Weigh yourself in the morning,
Get a blood test annually,
Chart your glucose and cholesterol,
Count calories, carbs, fat, protein, and fiber,
Change the batteries in your remote once in a while
Before you eventually sit down to dial up the favorite show
That you produce, direct, and cast the actors.

Don't forget to check the weather in major cities,
Mud, hurricane, tornado, and fire seasons,
Celebrate the summer and winter solstices,
Spring forward and fall back.
Record your systolic and diastolic pressures,
Know your bodily measurements, your BMI,
Count your blessings, bite your tongue,
Put your foot in your mouth,
Create your dreams,
Turn the lights on and off and on again.

Remember to water the lawn,
Write rhymes at dawn,
Know the difference between an I am and an iamb,
Pentameter and hexameter.
Don't be afraid to be a repeater,
Or pay the parking meter,
Because free verse is not as free
As you think it ought to be.

Believe that you are the master of your craft,
Can make your readers cry or laugh,
So when you practice the tricks of your trade,
Count your syllables and know what a metaphor is for,
How a simile is somewhat similar,
Like a facsimile that you fax
When you pay your income tax.
Let language be your thoughts
And thoughts be your language.

Learn what every word means, how to spell them,
Choose images that explode,
Motifs and themes to encode,
The difference between known, knew, and knowed,
When to hyphenate, to punctuate,
And when to alliterate,
Try to tackle ten total traits,
Emulate and deviate,
Even alienate
From the different movements and schools,
And intentionally break all the rules.

Question what life is about,
Speak your mind without doubt,
Not being too sentimental,
Boring, cloying, or experimental.
Your words can be novel without being a novel,
Not too archaic or overly prosaic.
Clichés have their days lots of different ways.
Place the speaker in the setting

Without forgetting images that
Hang with pushpins on the walls of your daydreams,
Not too flowery and nothing too annoying.

Try your hand at sonnets, sestinas, villanelles,
Odes, ballads, haiku, to name a few.
Read Shakespeare once again
And other famous poets, Google them.
Discover where poetry came from
And where you are going today with your verse
So that you can tell the difference between illusions and allusions,
Or else, when in the room the women come and go,
They will be talking about Leonardo.

Mix your drinks but not your metaphors
Because too many cooks break the camel's back.
Be precise with your ingredients,
Measure perimeters and parameters,
Acres, decibels, miles per hour.
Use Vernier calipers and check the PSI of your tires.
Don't confuse meters and milliliters,
Take out a ruler and compass so you don't get too lost.
Learn every angle on your protractor,
Every nook and cranny,
Every trope uncanny,
The pros and cons of self-critique.
Periodically check your speedometer and odometer,
Look over your shoulder,
Reset your clock to what you think is the right time,
Try to keep yourself out of trouble,

By adjusting the volume, bass, and treble.
To feel the energy and power of your poem.

Begin in a clandestine place after an alluring title,
An opening line the magnet for a flow of stanzas
That might evoke irony, a reflective symphony
That resonates with a variety of rhetorical devices.
Pay attention to word choices
That enhance the message and the meaning,
What the poem is really about,
Not distracted by slips in grammar and syntax,
Capitalization and apostrophes.

Have a good ear, choose your words carefully,
Sharpen your pencil, put in the time,
Read your poem out loud for several weeks,
Wake up and make changes until you're satisfied,
Then change it again so that maybe someday
You might show it to someone.
And after you've done all that,
All of the above and then some,
Thank your readers for the time they've been spending,
And reward them splendiferously with an effective ending.

Legere, Scribere, et Recitare

A palm is more than a tree
An open hand
A reader's lifeline and fortune
Hold it gently
Tightly
Let it guide you like a poem
And be what you want it to be

Geoffrey and Thomas

The librarian in the Rare Book Room
of the New York Public Library
showed me a hand-scribed incunabulum
of Chaucer's *Canterbury Tales*.

I read to her from the "General Prologue"
in Middle English,
we were both very young.

> *Whan that Aprille with his shoures soote*
> *The droghte of Marche hath perced to the roote,*
> *... And smale fowles maken melodye,*
> *That slepen al the night with open ye.*

Yes, it was April and raining,
   and the little birds chirped and slept with one eye open,
   while I went on an individual pilgrimage.

And she said, "If you want to see something really cool,
   we have a copy of T.S. Eliot's, "The Wasteland,"
   I knew, that's why I was there,
   but I couldn't check it out,
   too rare, but now it was here,
   on the original typing paper, with notes by Ezra Pound,
   unbelievable.

"April is the cruelest month, breeding
Lilacs out of the dead land, mixing
Memory and desire, stirring
Dull roots with spring rain."

And it was April again, spring break,
   the librarian wore white gloves
   and delicately turned each page for me.

These authors never knew each other,
   but both knew me,
   and gave me what I needed,
   without cruelty.

57th and 7th

I was born at the Osborne,
    an old luxury apartment building
    in the core of the Big Apple,
    rusticated brownstone cladding,
    catty-corner from Carnegie Hall,
    I recall falling down the steps
    in our small studio, slightly bruised and admonished.

My parents walked to the Stage for pastrami,
    corned beef at the Carnegie Deli,
    Leonard Bernstein a neighbor in glory,
    until we moved to our Upper West Side story,
    The Normandy, 86th and Riverside Drive.

Before graduating from college
    I sat behind Bob Dylan on the Carnegie Hall stage,
    my long hair flowing in a folding chair,
    blew my mind that I was there,
    the answer then was blowin' in the wind.

My next ticket the New York String Orchestra, costly
    on Christmas Eve in a blizzard,
    no buses running, no taxis,
    trudged more than thirty blocks up Park Avenue
    in the snow to take my girlfriend home,
    I slept in her parents' guest bedroom, mostly.

Years later the Vienna Philharmonic Orchestra,
    last row balcony with my wife
    and perfect pin-drop acoustics,
    we ate lunch at the Stage and the Carnegie
    before they closed for good.

The doorman allowed us into the Osborne lobby
    stuccoed and mosaic tiled walls,
    floors of varicolored Italian marble,
    glazed terracotta panels covering the ceiling,
    described in Wikipedia like "a luminous Byzantine dream,"
    for me simply melodies and memories.

Guppies, Rasboras, Neon Tetras, and an Angel, a Shakespearian sonnet

I told my Mom I only had one wish,
To use the money that was in my bank.
I hoped that she would let me buy some fish,
To keep them in my room inside a tank.
On Nassau Street with bright solariums,
Displays throughout resplendent, super nice,
Found rows and rows of cool aquariums,
A starter kit, five gallons, would suffice.
The gravel came in colors red to blue,
I had to buy a filter for debris,
A heater was another step to do,
The fish would rather go back to the sea.
At night I watched them swim around for food,
Transported, I was in a piscine mood.

In My Salad Days

I dressed peculiar,
Walked on parade in wing tips and white bucks,
Penny loafers with argyle socks,
Applied pomade by a stick to my crew cut,
Never used Brylcreem or Vitalis
To shape my pompadour or my restless spirit.

Dungarees and bell bottoms heralded relief,
Put me on the street,
Padded my pockets for the advent of adolescence,
Introduced me to each big adventure.
They all had cute names
And wore dresses,
Carefree, innocent, and ideal,
Teens dressed to the nines.

I was alive
Among tie dyed and flowered shirts,
A myriad of psychedelic colors,
Paisleys, reds, whites, and blues,
Fresh raw greens, shrooms, and some herb,
Oiled olive skin under see through blouses,
Beads and headbands,
Mixed, tossed, and seasoned.

Had I known then what I know now,
I would appreciate Caesar Cardini,
Who invented salad tableside,
One ingredient at a time.

Always Under Construction

I live my life
a work in progress
constant revisions
typos and misspellings
wishing I hadn't said what I did
I'm sorry I didn't really mean that
it came out wrong
too quick
my inner voice made public
just keep your mouth shut
nincompoop
buy some duct tape
visualize giving the middle finger
with both hands simultaneously
and then when you're alone in your car
driving down the backroads of your life
shout every curse word
you ever thought you knew
make up some new ones
loud and clear
until you can feel and hear
what peace and quiet sound like
In the vacant valleys of your ear

My Y Chromosome Causes Chaos, a ghazal

The phone will ring like wind chimes when female voices whisper,
Enticing sweet, subtle mimes when female voices whisper.

Alive in the twenty-third pair, a third the size of X,
And yearning for my hormones when female voices whisper.

Inherited from a father millions of years ago,
Bravado shouts out at times when female voices whisper.

Sensuous couples combine genetic information,
While mating during bedtimes when female voices whisper.

Births measured, counted, controlled by young sinners and old saints,
Strumpets share some love, not crimes, when female voices whisper.

Stereotypes confuse children, create myths and trauma,
Really hard on boys sometimes when female voices whisper.

Find your way along the twisted path of evolution,
Take care, mister, write some rhymes when female voices whisper.

Ambition

I can't do the butterfly
Dunk
Carry a tune
Understand the rules of cricket
Ski black diamonds
Dance the electric slide
The Macarena
Sew or iron
Cut my nails evenly

But I can
Tie a half and full Windsor
Make love with the lights on
Roast a Peking duck
Write a halfway decent poem
Roll a joint
Roll sushi
Take out the garbage
Search the internet
Work the remote
Fill up with gas
Buy groceries
Grill steak medium rare

What I can, I can
When I can

If I can
But what I cannot
I can't remember
If I can or cannot
So if I try, and can
Then I can
If not
I cannot
So why try if I cannot
Because maybe I could
And should try
Or not

The Fortunate One

I used to sleep at rest stops,
Stare at the stars and truck traffic,
Dozed more than once at a bus station,
Took a Thanksgiving turkey to a homeless shelter,
Friendly people in tents blessing me.
I was the fortunate one,
With a brokerage account and health insurance.

I smoked a joint in Greenwich Village,
Heard The Mothers of Invention at the Figaro,
Took the Staten Island ferry for a nickel,
And a derelict man to breakfast before Sunday School,
Bacon eggs and toast for his bloodshot eyes.
I was the fortunate one,
Put a few coins in the tzedakah box.

I rode the Andes Express from Cuzco to Puno,
Looked out the window at miles of flea market,
Everything from pots and pans to electronics,
Took a boat to a floating island in Lake Titicaca,
And a hydrofoil past warring villages to Bolivia.
I was the fortunate one,
Able to escape with Abercrombie & Kent.

I wrote letters to registered Democrats,
Urging them to vote for democracy,

Bought three hundred forever stamps monthly,
Watched the news daily,
And got shocked by the election result.
I was the fortunate one,
Living in a bubble at Del Webb Sun City.

I now only read headlines to stay informed,
Mourn for thousands killed in wars,
Wonder where the children will live,
And how the hospitals will function,
How women will control their bodies.
I am the fortunate one,
Old, retired, healthy, wealthy, and worried.

Special Effects

The set designer built a sun,
Colored the photosphere bright white,
Dressed me in a latex suit,
Dropped me in a field of artificial tulips,
And when the script called for gloom,
It started to rain.

I flew into the night and almost hit the moon,
Then the music got louder,
And sirens could be heard in the distance,
A touch of lightning and some thunder.

I fell in love with a latex woman
With perfect prosthetic teeth,
Walking on the beach
As it started to snow very light flakes
That we could catch in our mouths.

We were surrounded by talking animals,
Plushies with bows and ribbons,
A buffet table with plastic food
That tasted like air,
And an animatronic pot roast
That pranced around
Like a computer generated buffalo.

The sex scene was unbelievable,
We were both on top
As the lights dimmed,
Candles appeared,
And the subtitles
Were indecipherable.

The credits went on forever,
The casting director and music composer,
Hair and make-up artists,
Visual effects supervisor,
Editor and director of photography
The executive producer and the writer
Were all the same person,
Someone I knew very well.

The Day I Didn't Get a Tattoo

My back was out completely
Because I couldn't see it,
Also my face and neck,
No initials or anyone's name,
Slogans or sayings.
Color too expensive,
An artist difficult to choose,
Permanence oppressive.

I had a pierced ear for a week,
Maybe two, in San Francisco,
Never got past the stud,
Took it out and lost it,
Can't even remember which ear,
Gay or straight.

I'll just have to be satisfied
With a few moles and café-au-lait spots,
Scars from an appendectomy
And total knee replacements,
That can identify me,
Along with dental fillings,
In case I end up
In a ditch, or a canal,
Or some other final moment.

I could choose to pick a font,
And have one placed on my butt,
For all to read like the morning paper,
The obituary section,
No graphics, just letters, "The End,"
Or should it say, "Tail End, or "Rear End,"
One word on each cheek.
Too many decisions
For someone not usually indecisive.

By now all the parlors were closed,
The doors locked, the lights turned out,
My opportunity to ink dried up,
And I don't regret what I didn't do,
Devote my body eternally to a tattoo.

Mon Meilleur et Mon Pire Souvenir

The best French fry
I ever had
Was in Clécy
After kayaking the gentle Orne.

Spilling over *trois cascades,*
Losing my Oakley sunglasses
And drinking a cold Stella Artois.

Rafraîchissant at la guinguette
Across from *le moulin à vent,*
Now our *hôtel* for *le dîner,*
Avec un plateau de fromage
As large as our table.

I could choose my cheese,
Barely remembering a morsel of high school French
Suffered with Monsieur Ferdinand M. LaBastille,
A former spy and a cantankerous curmudgeon,
Reprimanding me daily, "Lyon, *idjot,*
Always clown around,
Step outside, I give you an 'E' for the day."

Emersion is clearly the best diversion,
The ultimate excursion,
That's it, nothing more,

Non, merci,
No thank you,
That's enough nostalgia
Before my polyglot brain gets myalgia,
Au revoir.

No One's Home

We sold our house in a minute
And all the crap that was in it
Who would want this stuff
We used it once
That was enough
Where we're going
We won't need it
Nothing needs to be repeated
We hadn't lived there very long
Empty now nothing wrong
Passed inspection
In compliance near perfection
So just remember
Some advice we once offered
Something that we said
That's your inheritance
When we're dead

Our Lives in a Whirlpool™

My plastic bottle of hoisin sauce
Stands tall dark and handsome
Next to my wife's dietic white tub
Of Chobani plain non-fat Greek yogurt.
We live side by side in our refrigerator freezer,
With a broken ice machine
That doesn't matter as it still makes ice,
Just doesn't dispense.
We're all getting older.

The cheese drawer has her low-fat mozzarella,
My Tillamook extra-sharp cheddar.
The deli drawer her sliced turkey,
My Boar's Head London broil cap-off top round oven roasted beef.
Her container of egg whites in the door,
My dozen extra-large, free-range, cage-free eggs on a shelf.
A bottle of her unsweetened almond milk next to my Topo Chico,
As we prepare to cook for dinner
Costco farm-raised fresh Atlantic salmon
Seasoned with S&P, Kirkland Signature EVOO, grilled to 145 degrees,
And served with vibrant green perfectly steamed organic broccoli,
Long-grain fragrant jasmine rice paddled from our electric rice cooker.

She eats her salad last with Gerard's 60 calorie champagne vinaigrette.
I prefer my salad first with Ken's Steak House raspberry walnut dressing.
She talks about the day when only one of us will be here.

I reminisce about how the pool was empty when I went swimming.
We wash dishes and put food away in unison
Before we top off the evening with Häagen-Dazs mango sorbet.
I have a bowl, she has a ramekin, 200 calories per serving.

The door to the fridge is opened and closed all day long.
Jack Spratt and his wife live together in there,
Somewhere between the chimichurri and the pro-biotics,
Listening to each other and holding hands, maybe in the freezer,
With homemade bran muffins and imported smoked salmon.
I try to stay regular while she maintains an anti-inflammatory diet.
We set the kitchen table with woven vinyl placemats,
Knives and forks or chopsticks and ceramic Japanese ramen spoons,
Along with a pair of Vanity Fair extra absorbent paper napkins.
While the world spins out of control, we live in our private bubble,
Share each meal talking about yesterday, today, and tomorrow,
Sometimes over brunch, sometimes for late lunch,
Always during dinner.

Our Dog Wears Diapers,
a rondeau

River is a rescue, she comforts us.
She eats and sleeps each day with little fuss.
We keep her off the carpet 'cause she pees,
Yet sometimes clean with Folex on our knees,
And try our best with humor not to cuss.

She's happy in our golf cart shuttle bus,
Arthritis meds at times that we discuss,
Mostly deaf though startled at every sneeze.
River is a rescue, she comforts us.

She bestows emotional support; thus,
Wearing cloth pads deemed not superfluous.
We feed her on a schedule to appease,
Take her to sniff the greenbelt as we please.
Every day she gives our lives a plus.
River is a rescue, she comforts us.

The Garden of Hedon

"I wandered lonely as a cloud"
— William Wordsworth

I joined the nudist colony down the street,
Got the senior discount right away,
Caught the early bird special,
All the ribs you can eat,
Fig leaves were a special treat,
Dining al fresco in the buffet.

The chocolate fountain sprang a leak,
The all-inclusive menu rather bleak,
Cheez Whiz and Velveeta,
Cool whip, deviled eggs, gluten free pita,
Organic apple sauce forbidden,
My naked body no longer hidden,
The staff thought the food quite good,
I found some dreadful flavors evil,
Avoided those considered lethal.

I met a self-made woman there,
Her charm totally serpentine,
Behavior that changed with every scene.
She handed me a fountain pen
To write an impassioned, lovesick poem
About the genesis of our first affair,

And asked for me to pardon her.
I told her I was waiting for the gardener.

My heart, with too much pleasure filled,
Limped carefully over the hill,
Encountered every kind of animal.
Tired and euphoric,
I crossed two rivers by a dam,
And eve descended with little thrill,
While I searched for a yellow daffodil,
My mind and gait unstable,
Without a cane and able,
To set it on an embalming table,
Smell it when it blooms
Before I get expelled.

I carved my initials on the tree of life,
Knowing what I knew of strife,
And had as much paradise as I possibly could,
Doing what I shouldn't while appearing as I should.
My bare body clothed my measureless mind,
As I left no traces of my journey behind,
Believing wholeheartedly to never say never,
Accepting the truth I would not live forever.

Postnuptial Agreement

My husband is the kindest thing,
Well not quite a thing but sometimes,
Not really an object but objectively speaking,
He speaks a lot of nonsense often,
But not for him, it's meaningful,
Even though I'm not really listening,
Though I pretend to be, nod my head and smile,
Look as pretty as can be,
Which is not always as easy as to agree
With everything he says,
When I can hear him
In the other room
Like a distant, random act of kindness,
An echo somewhere in my heart.

The Succubus

I met her first when I was young,
She asked my name, where I came from.
I could barely speak and held my tongue,
As she swept me with her silken broom.

She came to me every night,
Woke me with her siren song,
Played a flute into the moonlight,
Until steamy dreams were way long gone.

I went to bed waiting for her,
Left a space for her head on my pillow.
She never failed to stir my heart,
My body glowing, my breathing shallow.

She always held me in her arms,
Encouraged me to be a man,
Beguiled me with her sensuous charms,
Stroked me with her gentle moans.

She loved me softly in my sleep,
Held me closer to her breast,
Took me deeper into the deep,
Taught me how to hold my breath.

I look for her every day,
Reminded of dream after dream,
I listen for what she might say,
As we need each other as a team.

Shopping for Sex Toys

I found a vibrating wheelchair, a walker with attachments
A silicone cane, hypoallergenic and flexible,
Lotions, oils, candles, and lubricants,
Voltaren and arnica gel, delay spray, really?
Viagra, Cialis, digitalis,
Spanish fly drops, perfumed aphrodisiacs,
Bedrails, diapers, and urinals,
Waterproof sensory blankets, an anti-fatigue floor mat,
Stimulators and pill crushers,
Restraints and grab bars, handcuffs, collars, and leashes,
Knee, ankle, back, and wrist braces,
Ribbed condoms, French ticklers,
A trapeze above the bed,
"Makes getting up and down a lot easier,"
Compression socks, a handheld shower head,
Scented candles and nightlights to void bumping in the dark,
Lingerie and adaptive clothing, seductive videos and music,
Smart speakers for hands-free capability,
Talking clocks and watches to keep track of lost time,
Automatic shut-off safety devices, reachers and grabbers,
Ramps for entryways with steps, motorized scooters,
Rubber or plush anthropomorphic, anatomically correct
Stimulating blowup dolls anticipating the advent of talking robots.

The industry has gone geriatric,
Products for sex and old age all from the same company.
Dressed in a French maid's outfit
And wearing a platinum blonde wig,
The senior sales lady looked me over,
Asked for all my preferences and desires,
My age, history, and goals,
Told me what she liked the best, what works for her,
What I could try and test but could not return,
That I was not too old to love with zest, to enjoy every moment
As long as my heart was still throbbing in my chest.
She packed a large discrete box of all my purchases,
Charged my Visa card, wished me well, shook my hand,
And gave me a couple of free gifts,
A blood pressure monitor
And a personal alert system.

Hemorrhoid Surgery Kicked My Ass

Every day was interrupted
by dire lessons in perseverance
as I wore Depends for men
and took sitz baths
in the mouth of a volcano.

I am the exiled King of the Isles of Piles
my current throne a memory foam
blue velour donut pillow
where I count out Narcos tablets
to swallow around the clock
with Metamucil chasers
I chart grams of fiber
like mercenary soldiers
softening stools without mercy
and fighting a relentless war
in the bowels of Hell
dressing their wounds with gauze
and patting their cheeks dry
with Ultra-Soft Charmin.

Dealing with the monotonous
Rigorous routine of recovery
I've come to conclude again
that it's all a matter of perspective
a constant, yes, pain in the ass

that will pass like gas
as I lie awake for hours in bed
with the most depressing thoughts
that wrestle with each other
until my blood pressure machine
calls time out and asks to start anew
to try again, a do-over.

Pre-op, op, and post-op
tested, anesthetized, and traumatized
successfully repaired but wounded
I drop trou and kneel in prayer
bend over the examination table
as the anoscope peeks into my future
my rectum a wreck
refitted, restored, and renewed
to someday appear renovated
replete with new ideas
and hopes to conquer all movements
nervous worries and mental anguish
those dark thoughts that whimper
when I'm all alone and prone
in the middle of the night
buried in the sheets barely alive
and looking forward to being transported
to Kingdom Calm.

The Spiders on My Foot, a sestina

Their blood-pumping webs branched thin and weary,
On tired feet that left fragile footprints,
Stepped in oceans barefoot year after year,
Plodding forward, backward, sideways even,
Trying to decipher the sound of waves
And spread my tales with a humorous vein.

Now the blood burst darkest red from my vein,
Needing a towel and feeling weary,
My life gushing out a fountain of waves.
The tiled kitchen floor bore bloody footprints,
My past first-aid training kept me even,
In these moments that seemed more like a year.

Would I survive to live another year,
Trusting urgent care would shut off my vein?
My wife quickly wrapped the damage, even
Though the two of us were rather weary,
Growing old together, sharing footprints,
Living the ups and downs that came in waves.

This unforeseen crisis sounded like waves
Crashing through my skin from another year
When bleak thoughts of death left nasty footprints,

Like miners digging an immortal vein,
Their bruised hands and my foot sore and weary,
My mind and balance anything but even.

I thought I would bleed out and die, even
Putting pressure on spurts that came in waves.
Exhausted, drained, and becoming weary,
I limped into the car, it took a year.
My wife drove, I elevated my vein
While trying not to leave purple footprints.

The hospital was empty, no footprints,
The waiting room had no people even.
A nurse quickly called out to see my vein,
The doctor removed the wrappings in waves,
Said this was quite common every year,
He cleaned and sprayed, I became less weary.

I walked out with footprints like shallow waves,
Even though my valves were open this year,
Each varicose vein still very weary.

Calories, a villanelle

They creep around my waist like an abdominal thrust,
This invisible energy from the food I consume,
Keeping count of them with old age is a must.

I read about them on labels that I have to trust,
Advice from nutritionists that is correct I assume,
They creep around my waist like an abdominal thrust.

If I have too many I have to adjust,
Or I end up with pain on the floor in the bathroom,
Keeping count of them with old age is a must.

The desire to gorge is like gastronomic lust,
Their lure an enticing aromatic perfume,
They creep around my waist like an abdominal thrust.

If I overindulge my stomach will bust,
And my visage will be clouded with doom,
Keeping count of them with old age is a must.

Where will they go when I turn into dust?
Will they rest in peace when I lie in my tomb?
They creep around my waist like an abdominal thrust,
Keeping count of them with old age is a must.

An Everyday Occurrence, a limerick

I walk into the kitchen like wind I am blown,
As to what I came in for a great unknown.
I know that I'm on some kind of a mission,
But my memory is not in the best condition,
And I can't find my glasses, my car keys, or phone.

Witching Myself Good Luck

I took a forked stick into the forest,
Crossed my fingers, arms, and legs,
Listened for a tree to fall
And break the silence of the latest doldrum.

Deaths of parents, children, and friends,
Disillusioned dreams and fractured memories,
Searching for buried water to drown sorrows
And quench the drought of superstition.

I grabbed both ends, palms upward,
And walked along the path of myth, science, and religion,
Listening for messages and meaning,
Anything that would guide me forward.

Then I heard a voice,
Faint and fervent,
More than a whisper, less than whimper,
A presage I had not expected.

Leave the forest, leave the valley,
Pack up whatever hope you can,
Destiny is drying up, young man,
Break the stick, make a wish, do not dally.

The glimmer has nearly burst,
Hold on to what you know of thirst,
You may not be the last,
And surely you are not the first.

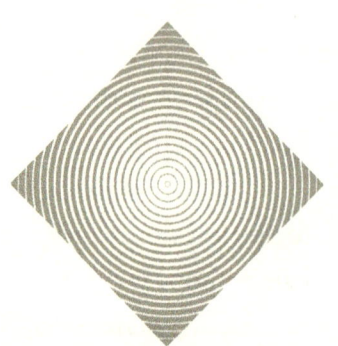

II

On Second Thought

October 7

There is no humor in a dead heart,
No music to dance in the desert,
No lines of poetry,
Tee shirts and dresses with festive colors,
No colors at all.
No hands to hold,
Lips to kiss,
Arms that hug,
Smiles that laugh,
Meals to share,
Or eyes that see everything bright.

Only silence,
Fear like darkness,
Unimaginable terror,
Cruelty more evil than evil,
Sounds that shouldn't exist,
And memories that shake the night.
Roll the darkness up into a tight ball,
And throw it against a blood-stained wall
With all your strength,
And try to believe in abundant peace,
Prayers to put you at ease,
When you mourn and never rest,
And never forget until you finally fall asleep.

Make Love Not War at The Pendulum, 1968

The stairs to the coffee shop were steep,
Tables covered in coarse burlap,
Wooden telephone wire spindles
Spread across a dimly candlelit room,
The coffee steeped in dented pots,
The conversations reached for something higher,
Good vibes, poetry, and pot,
Friday nights played a vital role,
In making meaning out of the Sixties.

> *Every day the news was scrolling*
> *Names of boys killed in Viet Nam,*
> *We made sandwiches for hungry students*
> *And tried to keep things relatively calm.*

The music lit up psychedelic posters,
The conversation cloaked in slogans,
Peace buttons and hand signals,
Signs of protest and desperation,
Marching in peaceful altercation,
Identified a changing culture,
Everyone waiting at the juncture,
Where they would depart for the future.

Every day the news was scrolling
Names of boys killed in Viet Nam,
We passed out pamphlets, "No More War,"
And posters, "Ban the Bomb."

Anti-establishment was the conviction,
Anything to get rid of Nixon,
We sat around tables telling stories,
Intimate conversations and sexual relations,
Not understanding the politics of war,
But knowing there had to be something more
Than anger, hate, and killing.

Every day the news was scrolling
Names of boys killed in Viet Nam,
Statistics more and more appalling,
We wanted peace, not another A-bomb.

We had to contend with the draft,
Life determined by lottery,
The system had gone completely daft,
Uncle Sam had made us property,
Yet we dug deep to find resilience,
Hoping that we would make a difference.

Every day the news was scrolling
Names of boys killed in Viet Nam,
We felt as if the sky was falling,
That no one really gave a damn.

Some dodged the draft and fled to Canada
Crossed the border by the thousands,
Packed their bags with cannabis,
And a barely meager allowance,
While others looked desperately for exemptions.

Every day the news was scrolling
Names of boys killed in Viet Nam,
Widows needed consoling,
Wanting the lion to lie down with the lamb.

The coffee was always hot and black,
Candles replaced with fresh enthusiasm,
The roast grew stronger as it percolated,
Filling the void with bitter sarcasm.

Every day the news was scrolling
Names of boys killed in Viet Nam,
Sadness filled the well-worn floor,
Until conviction ended the war.

Educating Disturbed Children

Winterode School, Crownsville State Hospital
Maryland, 1969-1971

I drew a large circle on the chalk board,
My forearm the radius of a compass,
Swinging clockwise with precision
Around my elbow, perfectly symmetrical as practiced.
My back to the handful of students
Committed to a hospital for the mentally ill,
Some locked in forensic wards like mad cattle,
Others bused in from schools that expelled them.
I wanted to explain circumference as $2\pi r$.

My first class as a novice teacher,
These teenage students introduced me
To the world of emotionally disturbed adolescence
By throwing a wooden desk across the classroom,
Breaking a lightbulb in a bare hand,
Unbuttoning the ruffled blouse of a fifteen-year-old blonde
Who had been a stripper on The Block in Baltimore,
And just sitting there smiling
After taking LSD every day for a year,
Robbing a gas station at fourteen, pregnant at thirteen,
Sleeping in a bathtub, and trying to commit suicide.
Psychotic, schizophrenic, and catatonic,
They could care less about pi.

What do you teach these children,
Who acted with no moral compass?
Certainly not math, who really cares about math?
You don't teach math, you teach children.
That's the ultimate lesson plan,
And never turn your back on them
When they walk traumatized into your classroom.
Look them in their dazed eyes and smile back.
They are who they are,
So show them how to learn,
And be what they can be.
Just believe that one day one of them will say,
"You bastard, you actually taught me to like math."
Teach them that they can achieve,
That they're smart,
And that someone truly cares about them.

Cease and Embrace

Don't kill them with words,
Slander, epithets and blasphemy,
Weapons that scream terror in the night.
Enough of fear,
Tears that never wipe away and dry.
Take to heart that you should love thy neighbor
And turn swords to ploughshares,
Let the lion lie down with the lamb.
Believe and make possible the impossible,
Adjust your attitude and preconceptions,
Step outside your former beliefs
To become a different person from what you were
So that you can embrace your enemies
And kill them with kindness.

May Day

My immigrant grandparents
Took some kind of boat,
Left their homelands for reasons
I will never know,
Though I've thought about leaving mine
On more than one occasion.

I know of those who have been abused
In one way or another,
Suffered through harmful relationships,
Dysfunctional families,
Or failed at various endeavors,
Questioned self-worth and confidence,
Cowered behind insecurity.

Should I send out a distress signal for them,
Call the hot line, the help line,
The crisis line, the life line?
I watch descendants of immigrants,
Worried for children and grandchildren,
Making final efforts before they give up.

Many carry on with pride,
Refuse to sound the horn,
Pull the fire alarm,
Wait until the almost very end,

When they can barely say the words,
With waning courage clouded in smoke.

I could try to help if they wish,
Find the support they need,
Take them out of their misery,
Get back on their feet.
I could make an urgent call,
In my desperate French accent, "*M'aidez.*"

Ecstatic Discovery and Tragic Recovery

– in respect of Butoh after World War II

Little Ushio found a dinosaur egg,
Proudly brought it to his mother for breakfast,
But couldn't find her in the kitchen,
The house was dark,
He was alone to make pancakes.
Pulling the flour from the pantry,

He covered himself in misery,
Danced to shake off his white coating,
Before the egg hatched
And devoured him.

His day not off to a good start,
Ushio decided to turn to art,
Dance away frustration with arms and legs,
Spooky unlike Kabuki,
Silently starving in his heart,
No longer interested in eating eggs.

Deeply engrossed in his new movements,
He suddenly heard something crack,
The shell exploded to his astonishment,
Grabbing a frying pan from the rack,
He cooked a Brontosaurus not very easy.

Pleased with his dilemma circumvented,
By his sunny-side-up repast invented,
A way to bring the past into a future scene,
With Mesozoic culinary haute cuisine,
That satisfied his hungry belly,
As he ruled the kitchen like Machiavelli.

Older Ushio licked his chops,
And looked around for a bottle of Schnapps,
To wash down memories of prehistoric time,
And move his body slowly like a sleepy rhyme,
That undulates and never stops
Until it has erased all crime.

Chicxulub

Look it up and you'll feel minuscule,
Astronomically little,
Tinier than a dinosaur's tear,
Long forgotten and dried up,
Not even fossilized.

If you look it up,
Which you will,
You will discover your vulnerabilities,
The accumulation of dispensable moments
That mean everything and nothing.

Just look up into the sky,
The stars,
What we call heaven,
And wonder what will happen next,
And if you will survive.

You might think that you're in control,
But you know that you're not,
Not by a long shot,
Not by a rock landing on your head,
Or something much worse instead.

In the Valley of Dead Stars

Five hundred million light years from earth,
She exploded in a dramatic supernova,
The sizzling end of her brilliant life,
Her hot light still visible if you look.

Turn left on Dinah Shore Drive
To see the U.S.A. in your Nova Chevrolet,
Head into McDonald's, order from the dollar menu,
A sizzing sausage biscuit for only three bucks.
Watch Coachella Valley couples checking the stars,
Reading their horoscopes and starving to death,
As they venture out for hot breakfast and a signature kiss,
Holding hands in their own private galaxies
On streets named after people they never knew.

In another universe twelve miles east of Palm Springs,
Enter Eisenhower Medical Center on Bob Hope Drive
With free valet parking and password protected MyChart messages.
Their board certified battalion will keep you alive
With the best doctors in the desert,
Nurses, schedulers, and hand sanitizer.
Get surgeries, blood tests, and images,
Slapstick, double-takes, and wise cracks,
Starbursts and a Milky Way in the gift shop.
Please come back in six weeks,
Pay for one liners to see how you're doing,

And when the doctor asks, just say,
"I don't feel old. I don't feel anything till noon."

Looks like Frank Sinatra Drive has been exterminated,
No more long-tailed, rat pack startled strangers in the night.
That's life in the desert encircled by lustrous country clubs
And dazzling casinos that advertise to Fly You to the Moon.
Monty Hall Drive enthusiastically tries to make a deal
With the California Skyway Patrol,
Tempting you to take the hidden curtain
Or the final mahogany box,
Before you get star struck, zonked, and end up imploded,
Somewhere in the neighborhood with your desolate soul lost in space,
In nearby proximity to the statue of Marilyn Monroe.

You can hear Gene Autry back in the saddle again,
Singing like a cowboy star gazing on his Trail to the airport,
As Bing Crosby Drive croons anything but "White Christmas,"
Not far from the illusion of Rancho Mirage and the Road to Singapore.
Danny Kaye also has stardom asphalt nearby,
Where the Court Jester, Geppetto, and Captain Hook
Are In good company with Greer Garson, Claudette Colbert,
Barbara Stanwyck, Burns and Allen.
Cruising in high gear, you can turn down Dean Martin Drive,
Go past Jack Benny and Marx Roads,
And steer onto the Sonny Bono Memorial Freeway
To get to wherever it is that you are determined to go,
Take photos and show people that you were there,
Trying to remember who was famous for what.

They were all once in the starlight, got old, drew a last breath,
Ran out of gas and either quietly faded away,
Or came back yesteryear as reruns and bygones.
Some tragically exploded, encouraging the birth of other stars,
To find fame or to otherwise obliterate themselves
Like the sun will do when the last lights go out.

My personal street continues to remain unnamed,
No gas lamps or signs to help star-struck tourists with directions
To find my monument of undiscovered concrete
Poured on loose, fragmented gravel, windy and circuitous,
Hard to locate in the daytime and even more elusive at night,
When barely asleep, I only radiate a little light.

Star light, start bright, I might not be the first star or street you see tonight.
I need to get polished, rubbed and repaved, repair my potholes,
Fill in the cracks, smooth out the wrinkles, make a wish.
At least my street accompanies me wherever I go,
Avoids pedestrian traffic, shooting stars, chaotic intersections.
I shine when I drive my sparkling Chevy Impala,
Fast and bold like the embodiment of living stars,
Luminous in my own imagination, celestial on rare occasion,
Even lustrous from time to time, alive and flamboyant.

I twinkle, twinkle with a billion trillion other stars,
Laid to rest, once headliners for Coachella Fest,
Some unknown and some forgotten,
Observable in the universe in and above the valley.
Every star has a name, every star looking for fame,
Or maybe it's just a game, a losing hand of solitaire to blame.

Like an eyeglass peering into the past to find the here and after,
I count the stars in the heavens, relishing whatever light they can create,
And every so often, if I squint, I see them clearly visible with my naked eye.
We are all-stars, shining or not, reflecting on the valley floor,
Living for a time in the spotlight, thinking about our futures,
And what we choose to do for now until we step out and finally disappear.

Bas Relief

Plaster visage on a wall trying to write dactylic hexameter,
Like Longfellow's *Evangeline*, Acadian girl searching for lost love,
Trying to imitate Greek and Latin classics, heartbroken but hopeful,
Unrhymed with varied skill and craft like Homer's *Iliad* and *Odyssey*,
Quarreling quietly in his thoughts like Agamemnon and Achilles,
On a journey like Odysseus back to Troy, a poet in the desert on an iMac,
Awake definitely much too early in the middle of the bleak night.
No forest primeval to comfort him with murmuring pines and hemlocks,
Rather desert oasis, Bermuda grass, bougainvilleas, variety of cacti.
Winds blow sand every which way believing patience will shape the words
And deliver them from lost sleep into a poem, an embodiment
Of tradition and future, standing on its own in grief and happiness.

We the People

I. A Perfect Union

I look at photos of members in Congress,
They all excelled at something,
School leaders and debaters,
Veterans, board members, and city council,
Dress themselves in white-collar clothes,
Wear a pin or a flag,
And try to smile a smirk for the camera.

They speak in political jargon,
How they were taught to argue,
And what they pretend to believe,
What their followers want to hear,
Constituents younger and older,
Not really knowing what they voted for.

They gather to deal with convoluted issues,
Having limited understanding of the impacts,
Timelines and rules,
Just follow the leader,
Ask for what you need,
And eventually compromise and concede.

II. Establish Justice

I went to Superior Small Claims Court
To sue an unlicensed contractor
Who wrecked our concrete overlay.
The driveway had to be demolished,
And even though he didn't show,
I won the full judgment.
Sitting in the crowded courtroom
With my cell phone turned off, couldn't talk,
Had to stand and raise my right hand,
Swear to tell the truth.
I looked around at nervous plaintiffs and defendants,
Wondering if they had their paperwork together,
Would speak up to tell their version of the truth,
In our letter-of-the-law litigious country
With the most legal proceedings on earth.

I question why our defendant didn't show,
Why he has not paid me or made a payment plan,
Why I have to serve him with a subpoena?
Did he intentionally not follow the law,
Disappeared or left the country,

(more)

Didn't believe in the Constitution,
Or want to be considered one of the compliant people,
Never voted or watched the news,
Has no conscience?
Was he just not willing to follow the norm?
Where did he go, to some immoral, unethical place,
Run for school board, city council, or Congress.
Did he even register to vote,
Or just make excuses day in day out,
Did his elders teach him to be that way,
Or does he just not care, vanish into thin air,
That really isn't as thin as his despair?

The robotic judge has seen it all before,
Signs the forms like a barista putting names on cups.
The bailiffs and the clerks get their pay,
And the mediators try their best to save the day,
As we all walk cautiously down the hallway,
Under the shadow of a bald eagle,
And do as best we can because we are the people.

Hold the Phone

Absolutely No Soliciting

Instead just send a fax with the facts,
I might accept a minimal few except for some.
I'd rather be allowed to read your offerings aloud,
You're just too annoying with your intruding contacts.

So if you call my cell to sell,
I'll say bye-bye and will not buy
From your callous voice, a callus on my brain,
Your tone too coarse, of course, as well.

Your irritating acts will ultimately get the ax,
Your coercive intents way too intense.
I knew that you were nothing new,
I've often seen this scene before, an anticlimax.

So build a plan for someone else to be billed,
Your enterprising bazaar is much too bizarre.
Your noxious feint has made me feeling faint,
And I find you should be fined and unfulfilled.

To be fair I know you need to charge a fare,
Do your job and earn what's due,
But you should refrain from being a pain in the butt,
So please hear what I'm saying here and take care.

When Billionaires Go Home

i.

They put on their pajamas,
Dismiss the valet,
Pay the wine steward,
Give orders,
Count their money,
Check the burglar alarms,
The market,
Their investments,
The mooring for their yacht,
Set the Nespresso machine timer,
Feed their pets,
Put out clothes for tomorrow,
Turn all phones to Do Not Disturb,
Take a poop,
Take a sleeping pill,
Wear a sleep mask.

ii.

The other thousands
Set up tarps under an overpass,
Sip cold drip coffee bought at a 24/7 convenience store
To use the restroom,
Wash their faces in the sink

With cold water that shuts off every five seconds,
Count panhandled coins and crumpled bills,
Check tomorrow's weather hot, cold, or wet,
Organize items from the food bank
In a borrowed grocery cart,
Cold meals that they can eat
Before they try to sleep
On a pad if they have one,
On the ground.

iii.

Many read and recite every single psalm and scripture.
What the hell is wrong with this picture?
It hangs on a wall with no ceiling or floor.
I'm pissed off that I can't do more,
Change what's wrong with this place.
Still, I sleep on a Helix mattress pillow top,
Go to ATMs and withdraw RMDs from IRAs.
I'm one of more than eight billion people,
Scattered like birdseed in air wherever I look.
Same old same old repeats itself ad nauseam,
Life flows on like an IV drip.
Blessings cannot be counted with truths and lies,
Until we finally lock our door and say goodnight.

just asking

are you all right
I'm fine
can you breathe
I can
can you walk
I will
what's the matter
nothing

how's your life
good
any issues
none
family ok
they're great
finances
no problems
medical bills
all paid

exercise
this morning
relax
this afternoon
sleep well
tonight
housing
comfortable
shopping
convenient
your car
in good shape
romance
loving

truth
not always

The Last Chapter, a *chastushka*

Authors try to pen a climax,
The protagonists are spineless,
Every book is lacking syntax,
Plots repeat themselves so timeless.

Scribes get lost in their nascent themes,
Tables of contents and settings
Dribble on poorly in reams,
Murder, lust, love, and beheadings.

Each attempt like an accouchement,
As the antagonists go home,
Characters find their denouement,
Just some words buried in a tome.

The Maven, a parody

Once upon a daytime sunny, with an awful cold, my nose was runny,
I needed to buy prescription medications at the store.
As I sniffled, barely breathing, coughing, gasping, loudly wheezing,
The telephone rang, rang, and rang incessantly like it had never done before.
Who is calling, I wondered, maybe someone asking for a chore,
Pestering me whatever for.

Ah, what a tormenting bummer in the silent dead of summer,
As I staggered laboriously from the kitchen through the corridor,
Hoping that the phone would stop as I had to go and shop
To get relief and maybe something more,
For my head was throbbing and my body sore,
Ready to collapse and fall to the floor.

The constant ringing gave my brain a stinging,
Wracked my body throughout every pore.
Exhausted, I tried to plug my ears, rid myself of nervous fears,
Praying the blasted phone would stop and ring no more.
I screamed and yelled and loudly swore,
"Hang up, damn it, and call no more."

Then I summoned all my courage, thinking the caller I could discourage,
And picked up the phone planning to beseechingly implore
This nuisance to recognize my illness and preserve some stillness,
And cease the shrillness that had shaken me to the core.
"Hello," I said, "What, for heaven's sake, are you calling for?
Leave me alone and don't call this number anymore."

Listening for a response, shuddering, thinking I could hear some stuttering,
Trembling, sweating, anticipating sudden candor,
Eventually the silence ended, but my heart was barely mended
When I distinctly heard the words, "Do not snore."
Who was this obnoxious person who told me not to snore?
How did they know what I did abhor?

I slammed down the phone, suffering at home all alone,
But soon I heard the ringing much louder than before.
The phone was clanging off the hook, causing me to take a look
To see if there was a crook observing at my backdoor.
I shivered knowing this was something I could not ignore,
Like being hit over the head with a two-by-four.

"Hello," I said again into the receiver, fearful of an artful deceiver,
Who was this noxious Maven whose presence had caused me pain for sure,
And delivered much annoyance, did he have clairvoyance,
That resounded with flamboyance as he loudly swore,
Singing like a virtuoso throughout my house, a demonic troubadour,
Repeating ad nauseum the message he'd said afore.

This know-it-all encouraging my feeble state of mind discouraging
By telling me what I needed not to do at night behind my door,
Though I was shabby and unshaven, behaving like a craven,
And deeply bothered by this Maven
Whom I truly did abhor.
Said the Maven, "Do not snore."

Now I wondered how this invective person, much like a detective,
Knew about my nightly behaviors just like a bore

Pushing the Limits

Who keeps track of things inconsequential listing them sequential,
Disregarding any potential that might encourage me to soar,
A person who understands my ins and outs, furthermore,
But only admonishes, "Do not snore."

Now this Maven, quite distinctly, talked to me succinctly
With three words to navigate my sleep ailments to the drugstore,
And not stop anywhere in between, nor do anything to cause a scene,
Just buy a CPAP machine like millions of others had done before,
And don't even think, though you have lots of phlegm, to purchase a cuspidor.
Said the Maven, "Do not snore."

I thought long and hard about his advice, knowing I had paid the price
Of sleep apnea that kept me awake in days of yore,
Tossing and turning in my bed with turbulent dreams racing through my head,
I knew that I would end up dead with pajamas that I never wore
And have nothing left in my heart, spirit, and soul to account for
Unless I heeded his monotonous refrain, "Do no snore."

Still the Maven continued clearly to castigate me sincerely
That I needed to gather my cash and head directly to the store.
Though his voice was rather prickly, and I still felt very sickly,
I got dressed extremely quickly and bolted for the door,
Taking the bull by the horns like a fervent matador,
To never hear again in my nighttime arena, "Do not snore."

I walked down the avenue lightly, though my visage was unsightly
As I passed by Walmart and a discount liquor store.
The pharmacist was officious, the outcome looked propitious,
My desire quite ambitious as I aimed to please my nagging mentor

Who had berated and harangued me o'er and o'er
With his dictum, "Do not snore."

I would soon get my equipment, in two weeks would be the shipment,
I also bought capsules, tablets, and a suspension of Cephaclor.
I would kill my cold with mixology before it took its toll on me,
And then deal with the idiosyncrasy that was responsible for my snore.
But first with food, every four hours, swallow the meds I had asked for,
And try not to think of the Maven saying, "Do not snore."

Back at home totally exhausted but once again accosted
By the phone that resounded with a cacophonic score,
Again a tone that pretended understanding but continued reprimanding,
The order sternly demanding that all options I explore,
That I try various concoctions, alter my life unless wanting to be done for.
Opined the Maven, "Do not snore."

My state of mind was shaky and my metabolism achy,
Exacerbated by his so-called words of understanding that on my conscience wore.
I tried to do some reading to help my mind from bleeding
And to discourage desolate thoughts from succeeding as I'd never done before.
I thus perused the pages of "The Tell Tale Heart" by Poe, who died young in Baltimo
Yet, somehow I could hear the Maven's message ever louder, "Do not snore."

Regretfully, my guilt I could not conceal as I suffered this ordeal
And thought about when my solitary life would be nevermore,
When I would disappear without a sound and be buried underground,
No longer be around, encapsulated in a coffin like a humidor.
I needed to escape my fate and exit my anxiety through a trapdoor,
To no longer hear the Maven pounding, "Do not snore."

Eventually, my CPAP arrived and I relished that I had survived
The ghastly torture and torment that was the source of all this uproar,
The disorder of my sleep that had left me in a heap
With my breathing stopping deep, now I finally did restore.
My comportment had ultimately returned to a semblance I could truly adore,
And never again hear those words, "Do not snore."

Multiple Choice

1. The pressure to perform was dominant,
    a) a furrowed brow and sweating palms were prominent
    b) find a way to leave the continent
    c) his attitude was predominantly petulant
    d) the performance was particularly reminiscent

2. The scene brought back feelings of insecurity,
    a) recollections and nightmares that lived in perpetuity
    b) theatrical presentations of obscurity
    c) raw emotions that needed healing
    d) post traumatic symptoms running rampant

3. The lighting was too dim to see expression,
    a) the sound too soft to hear the silence
    b) clouds were overshadowed with depression
    c) the animals were restless in the forest
    d) someone forgot that this was very frightening

4. Every gesture scrutinized by examination,
    a) finding a way for retaliation
    b) every motion sorely analyzed
    c) search for a way to leave the nation
    d) and suffering from contamination

5. Wouldn't you much rather fall in love?
    a) than feel the pressure of insecurity
    b) or not be able to see an expression
    c) and be restless in a forest of examination
    d) none of the above

Attack of the Mutant Ninja Similes

This poem is like a heart attack
A cardiac arrest as unexpected as a tsunami
Pouring thousands of gallons of water over the page
Like Alfred Hitchcock's *The Birds*
Flying willy-nilly like Willy Nelson's songs
Like "Mamas Don't Let Your Babies Grow up to Be Cowboys"
Or Glen Campbell's *Like a Rhinestone Cowboy*
Wearing Stetsons and stirrups like a Nashville fashion show
Walking the runway like Twiggy
Almost invisible like figures of speech
That eat metaphors for dinner
Gushing out of their mouths like a damn ruptured dam
That gets posted on Facebook with more than a thousand likes
Overused as a broken record broken record broken record
That rattles your brain like a freight train
Carrying a cargo of similes like this poem
That has at least a dozen
On purpose with humor like a monotonous comedy club

Happy as a Clam at High Tide

Safe from humanity for now,
My close relatives live at the bottom of Puget Sound
Clustered on old shells in brackish water
With an accumulation of organic and inorganic material,
Soil particles and decayed plant and animal matter,
Temporarily at peace on the seafloor.
Whereas, I am very lucky to be protected by waves
On an inter-tidal coastal beach

An outspoken leader of the Benthic community,
I remember my past and can only imagine my future.
Otherwise, I'm very sedimental.
My life is cluttered,
Most of my nefarious friends lack backbone,
Sea anemones, sponges, corals, sea stars,
Sea urchins, crabs, and an assortment of other eccentric characters.

I never say, "The world is my oyster,"
Even though I will be prepared on a kitchen counter,
A Formica slab in an epicurean mortuary,
In the hands of gourmet chefs,
Showering me with olive oil, minced garlic, lemon juice, and white wine.

I am a clandestine, glam razor clam
With no head or eyes,
Not Kosher, no scales,

But my mind is razor-sharp,
Until I get steamed up.
Even though I have a hard shell,
Shucks, I will get purged
And spit out grit in my final moments,
To enter bivalve heaven as a culinary delight,
The main course of an elegant dinner party,
Sprinkled with parsley and garnished with lemon wedges,
Served over a bed of angel hair pasta
For some fortunate family's gastronomic pleasure.

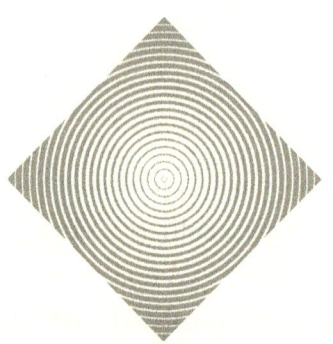

III

At Peace

The Extraordinary Escapades of Lilly and River

Lilly's a runner,
    found on the streets of Desert Hot Springs,
    rears her head back
    and howls like a wolf
    for no reason that we know,
    but she does.

She wears a YIP Smart Tag
    that tracks her meandering four minutes late,
    an Elizabethan collar when she got spayed.
We put "Please Close" signs on all the gates,
    only let her out with a leash,
    give her a bully stick at night to watch TV.
She has taken me on her journey,
    has become part of mine.

Her forerunner River went to the other side
    last April after a seizure,
    also a poodle rescue with her own unique stride,
    abandoned on Riverside Drive in Chino,
    almost dead, hair matted, covered in fleas,
    life-threatening pyometra, ovaries and uterus removed,
    seven years later mostly deaf and blind.
I keep her plaster paw print on my desk,
    touch it every day,

talk to her,
use her name for passwords.

My adventure began on the streets of Manhattan,
    86th and Riverside Drive,
    learned to walk on Broadway,
    crashed a two wheeler in the park beside the Hudson,
    avoided as many bullies as I could,
    navigated all the back alleys,
    like Allen Ginsberg in "Howl."

My two brave poodles, both cotton ball cloud white,
    saved themselves with all their might,
    lived alone with fright and flight.
All three of us learned to disappear with dreams into the night,
    find intuitive ways to escape,
    turn our lives into different shapes.

I wake up at three
    and try to figure out
    who I want to be,
    a lily of the valley,
    or a flowing river,
    write something meaningful that I can deliver.
The rest of you get up early and plan your day,
    deal your best any old way,
    you know your time here will not stay,
    that someday you will go away.

Now I run with Lilly,
   hear and see with River.
Losing a dog is more than hard,
   we said we would never get another pet,
   yet knew what we said was like a vignette,
   always changing over time.

So we paint our canvas every day,
   sketches and drawings vibrant in different ways,
   as we try to look at life like the artist
   who would brighten the portrait of a mourner
   by adding a little white dog in the corner.

Skipping Stones

You have to find the right one,
A billion years old,
Flat on both sides
Like a flounder,
With both eyes on the same side,
Or a silver dollar
With Lady Liberty on the front
And an eagle on the back.
Flip the stone in your hand a few times,
Feel its weight,
Call heads or tails,
Bend your knees,
And let it fly.

If you live in the city,
You have to find a river or lake.
Stones don't skip well on concrete,
But pink Spalding balls do just fine,
Playing handball and foursquare,
Stickball in the alley,
Punchball on the sidewalk,
Avoiding elderly women and parked cars,
A fire hydrant for first base.
Just make a fist,
And let it fly.

Every day becomes another stone,
Flat, round, or ragged
Tossed into whatever floats,
And destined to be sunk
Until all the waters dry up
And someone picks it from the pile,
Examines its features
And decides to give it praise
And let it fly.

Some stones don't skip,
Sink like a rock to the bottom,
Kerplunk and just disappear.
Some skip once, high and mighty.
Others twice, three, four, five, or more.
The last stone a final endeavor,
Keeps on skipping, skipping forever.

Stairs to the Ocean

Always more difficult going down
Than climbing back up,
Tattooed youth in flip flops scamper
While I hang onto the rail,
One step at a time.

Led Zeppelin keeps me moving,
Singing all that glitters is gold,
Makes me wonder about this stairway
And the bikini thongs with surfboards
Playing games in throngs at Solana Beach.

When I got to the sand the ocean flat,
Little children with shovels digging away,
Families with tents serving sandwiches
As the wind blew everything every which way
And the surf pounded the shore.

Enthralled and also in dismay,
Catching my breath for the next foray,
My progressive lenses gave me a different view,
Nothing was old and nothing was new
As I pretended to be exhilarated climbing back up the bluff.

The End of Travel

The last time I was in Mumbai was never,
A day after Karachi
And two weeks before Djibouti.
My passport had expired,
My picture out of date
Shaved my beard and mustache,
My plane arrived too late.

I am stuck on the tarmac of eternity,
Counting the crushed stones under my feet,
Friends who have aged out,
Or just disappeared, expired from social media.
Consumables in the cupboard,
I can't find where I put them
Where I've left my phone,
Or why my calendar resembles an encyclopedia.

My financial consultant
Said I would step out at ninety-seven,
That my portfolio allocation
Was a little rich,
Slightly out of balance
Son of a bitch,
So I infused Meyer lemons in 80 proof Smirnoff for limoncello.

The good news is that I'll never need
A colonoscopy again, imbibe another drop of Golytely,
Or try to figure out where I put the tickets,
Keys to locked suitcases, and expired scopolamine patches.
I won't have to deal with TSA and security
On this last embarkation to an inward destination,
Better than a Viking Cruise or Carnival Line.
I have captured the deadline and made it mine,
Wrapped my arms around elapsed time,
Boarded the terminal of the sublime,
All set, ready to go, and feeling just fine.

Lithe or Deaf

Defying leaps and sounds,
Like tripping over throw rugs
And throwing out the garbage,
Recycling cartons and reminders,
Hindrances and other body parts.

Listen to the signals,
And follow the script,
Not all that well equipped,
But eager to please,
And pleased to be beleaguered,
In a league of your own
With no sound in this zone.

Step lightly heel to toe,
Go to places that you know
And other spaces where you can grow
Into something else that's just for show.
Take a bow and nothing more,
Do it now while you have the chance,
You won't be called for an encore
As this, alas, is the last dance.

Everything Hurts

The moon beams
As the sun burns
Water soaks
And rocks slide

There's no place to hide
When the earth spins
It's not a hoax
Just the turn of the tide

So stay out of trouble
Seek peace in your bubble
Secure on the safe side
Humble with the struggle

Find a soft cushion
Drink an infusion
Enjoy what you can
Until the conclusion

A Date with Dr. Schnaser

My poor right knee is bone on bone,
Limping I tend to favor it.
Take Meloxicam at six each night,
Developed a gnawing crave for it.

I see the PA first week of February,
And will definitely not commit perjury
When I share the truth about my pain
And plead my case for surgery.

At night, I doze on my recliner with an ice pack,
Voltaren cream gives me relief for an hour.
I count the days and cross them off my calendar
Until my next appointment at Eisenhower.

The plan is to have a robot-assisted implant.
Hopefully, my orthopedic surgeon, a renowned iconic,
Will revitalize me as I grow older,
Becoming more and more bionic.

So, when my time comes like everyone else,
The plug, someone will have to pull it,
Though for now, I wait for a slight reprieve,
Remain calm and bite the bullet.

Why Not Complain

My mantra isn't working
I have to kvetch
What a bitch
I don't know who to call

Am I after hours
In a real emergency
Or just whining
When things don't go my way

No one wants to hear me gripe
They have their own laments to grumble
Don't care to know my nagging rumble
Grousing like a guttersnipe

Yet complaining is therapeutic
Gets the problems off my chest
Feelings interpreted like a hermeneutic
Spoken once and laid to rest

The Private Thoughts of Justin Time

He wondered if he would ever win,
Hold a plastic trophy to his chin,
Get accolades from a beauty queen,
A check for several hundred million.

Not be worried about what clothes to put on,
Write unique lyrics and carry a tune,
Cut his nails like in a salon,
Not be called a moron.

Finish something that he started,
Like this poem has him startled,
Searching for thoughts that are throttled,
And rhymes that make him bothered.

He tried to find his birth certificate,
Would not be alive without it,
Hung his only mirror in the closet,
Made his final bank deposit.

Every day another challenge,
Every minute takes revenge,
Each hour that he spends
Checked off on his calendar until the end.

Just Us and Our Stuff

Double, double toil and trouble;
Fire burn and caldron bubble.
— Shakespeare, *Macbeth, 4.1*

In our private bubble with little trouble,
The world around us crumbles,
Sirens sound daily
In the melee
Where people sleep in bedlam,
If they can sleep at all.

Yet, we have power recliners,
Fiber-optic cable TV,
Cell phones with Siri and 5G,
Organic meals on the table,
Hot water in the shower.
What could go wrong
Within this magical song?

Perennial ryegrass overshadows Bermuda,
Bare around the edges,
But who really cares?
Wild birds feast on Meyer lemons,
And we cook curd for bars,
Dust them with powdered sugar,
To sweeten the future.

Pushing the Limits

The world surrounds us, stumbles,
Closing in, upsetting our stomachs.
What can we do to not live our lives in chaos,
A nebulous existence amidst free will, fate, and prophecy,
Clouded with reminiscences of the past?
Everything is the same everywhere in every country,
The mundane has taken over the macro and micro,
Whether Canada Dry Zero Sugar in America
Or Crabbie's Alcohol Free Ginger Beer in Scotland,
Ginger ale reminds us of real ginger ale.
Avocados from Mexico are inexpensive, for now,
Especially when they're ripe,
Yet, the global news gets old and spoiled,
Tragedies, sour and rotten,
Recycled every Monday like stubble
With the rest of the trash.

I heat the wok on high,
Weave in some mystical ingredients,
Stir fry deveined, tail-off Argentinian shrimp,
Raw, not boiled or baked,
Add sweet onions and minced garlic,

No eyes of newts or toes of frogs,
Some baby bok choy, shiitake mushrooms, extra firm tofu,
Carrots and celery sliced on the diagonal,
Sai fun noodles and low sodium soy sauce.
This powerful broth will become a charm,
Remove the daily rubble, visions of all unsightly weeds,
When served with hoisin and toasted sesame seeds.

We sit down to feast surrounded by our belongings,
Only the two of us and a collection of remnants,
A solitary candle on the table,
Quietly looking out the window,
Pathway lights on a timer,
As are the sunset and the stars.
We are thankful that we can be thankful,
Talk about gratitude and what comes next.

Yet and yet and yet,
In the very final act,
I will speak out loud like the king of his clan,
"Tomorrow and tomorrow and tomorrow,"
Alone in his soliloquy
After the death of his distraught and overwhelmed lady,
Tormented by her past, a "damned spot" of guilt.
I will repeat it over and over and over
Until there is no tomorrow,
When all time ends,
And all brief candles go out.

The Great Wall at Badaling, 1983

I drove a Phoenix bicycle across Tiananmen Square,
The Eagles singing on my SONY Walkman,
"Welcome to the Hotel California."
The portrait of Chairman Mao looked solemn,
Hanging at the entrance to the red-walled Forbidden City.

They paid me as a Foreign Expert,
Gave us a third-floor flat at *Youyi Binguan*,
Beijing's Friendship Hotel built by the Russians in the 50's.
Two bedrooms, a methane tank for cooking,
Our mail was opened and our phone tapped,
Could always hear someone breathing on the line.
When we arrived, our jet-lagged sons constructed a labyrinth of LEGOs
And watched cockroaches try to find their way out.

I had coupons for white rice
And stuffed dumplings in the faculty cafeteria,
Which I ordered by the *jin*,
500 grams boiled then fried over hot coals
On a fifty-five gallon steel drum.
A worker asked how many potstickers I ate,
Then told me I made a good contribution to agriculture.

A section of the Great Wall from the Ming Dynasty
Loomed strategic and commanding,
Protecting the *Juyongguan* Pass

From barbarous northern invaders,
But not western bourgeois decadence,
Our celebration of Halloween,
And requests for soft beds and cold drinking water.

We climbed steps in our blue Mao jackets,
Wore caps with red plastic stars,
Bags of roasted peanuts in our pockets,
Feeling the friendship from curious communists,
Who dropped candy wrappers on the ground
And tried to understand our Mandarin.

As ambassadors of peace and good will,
Identified and welcomed as foreigners,
With big noses and peculiar habits,
We found safety and friendship behind parapets together,
Shared meals, music, a mutual sense of humor
That opened our eyes and removed walls.

Ten Days in the Holy Land, 2007

"We have no place else to go." — Golda Meir

Blown up at a bus stop in West Jerusalem,
Shimshon carried on a stretcher
Like a body of blood turned to stone,
Shown around the world by CNN.
A Jew born in Palestine
Before Israel existed,
Spoke Hebrew, English, Aramaic, and Arabic,
A former soldier and our private guide,
Everyone knew him by name,
And he knew all of Israel
Intimately like a groom knows his bride.

He embraced us at the Tel Aviv Airport,
Drove by van to the Jerusalem King David Hotel,
Where David took care of us in luxury,
Better than he took care of Goliath.
Shimshon designed our itinerary,
What he believed we needed to see,
Meeting his wife at their home for tea,
Everything he knew about his country.

The Muezzin called Muslims to prayer
Five times a day over speakers
Mounted on the higher part of the mosque's minarets.

Later we remembered the Holocaust at Yad Vashem,
A cattle-car headed to the gas chambers,
Patches with a star of David for identification,
Artifacts of the Warsaw ghetto, a display of shoes
From one-and-a-half million children,
The journey to all the death camps.

At the Mount of Olives, a Palestinian community,
The ancient city of Judah overlooking churches,
Mosques, and a Jewish cemetery,
A young beggar took all the coins from my open hand.
Photos in front of the Knesset,
Posing before a bronze, fifteen-foot menorah at the entrance,
A symbol of Israel's sovereignty and eternity,
Testament that we were there.

The Dead Sea Scrolls under glass
The Shrine of the Book, underground,
A white dome shaped like the jar lid
Where the scrolls were found.
Breathtaking stained-glass Chagall windows
In the synagogue of the Hadassah Hospital,
Providing care for Jews, Muslims, and Christians.
Vivid blues, reds, greens, and yellows,
Biblical motifs portraying the Twelve Tribes,
The sons of Jacob, recounting sadness,
A tribute to the millions of vanished Jews.
That night we caught our breath, realized our Jewishness,
Pita, hummus, olives, wine, and King David.

We climbed steps through the ancient irrigation system
Patrolled by young soldiers brandishing assault rifles,
A labyrinth of hidden passages in the desert,
Tunnels carved through solid rock,
Water channeled from the Gihon Spring,
Aqueducts to sustain life,
Pools for ceremonial purification,
Faith, miracles, and survival.
Shimshon bought us bottled water.

The Christian, Armenian, Muslim, and Jewish Quarters of the Old City,
Thousands of years of human history,
The festive Muslim Quarter celebrating Eid
With music and vibrant colors,
A packed restaurant made a place for us
To share falafel and French fries with our family.

A vacant room, the site of the Last Supper,
The first day of Passover,
Exodus from slavery in Egypt,
Freedom, bread, wine, no matzoh,
Twelve apostles denied betrayal,
Jesus washed their feet,
Judas should have washed his hands clean.

Following the path of Christ through narrow alleyways,
Touch His handprints on limestone walls,
Like plaster of Paris kindergarten art.
We stood restricted before the Al-Aqsa Mosque.

Muhammad transported from Mecca,
Whispered in my ear it would be all right
If I entered, people are people.
We walked one religion to the next
With no apparent boundaries,
No persecution or defamation,
Centuries of history, crusades, and conflict,
Destruction and crucifixion,
Tourists taking snapshots.

Prayed at the Wailing Wall,
Men separated from women,
A booth of Orthodox Jews
Selling plastic phylactery and slips of paper
To write a note or a wish
To wedge into the cracks of the ancient blocks,
Reciting Psalm 79, head bent, eyes closed,
"We are objects of contempt to our neighbors,
Of scorn and derision to those around us."

The open market a labyrinth of tables
Piled high with figs, walnuts, and pomegranates,
Bricks of halva like the stone walls of the city,
Vanilla, pistachio, dark chocolate,
Toasted coconut, cardamom,
I went for marble, manna from heaven.
Everyone in the market knew Shimshon,
Proud that every Jew in Israel had eaten halva,
He took an orange from a friend's table to share.

Lights flickered and frantic men in beaver hats
Sounded plastic *shofarim* to close all booths
Before sundown, or else.

A drive through alleys of Mea Shearim, home to insular Jews
Living with their ancestors,
Ultra-orthodox men racing through the streets
Wearing black hats and long coats
Their *payos* and *tzitzit* flapping as they darted home
Almost airborne like a cartoon in time for the sabbath.
Their wives in long dresses, hair covered with scarves and wigs,
Preparing dinner and tending to the children.
Our Shabbat Kosher buffet at the Kind David,
A challah at every table, brisket, fish, Israeli salads,
Prayers, chants, and silent meditations,
Lighting candles and thanking God
For the fruit of the vine and the bread of the earth,
A ritual alive in the past and present simultaneously.

Shimshon drove us past Bedouin camps
Scattered on the hillside from Jerusalem to Jericho,
Where the walls came tumbling down,
Descendants from Arabian desert nomads,
Raising animals with steadfast perseverance,
A strong determination to stay on the land.
Medjool dates through the Jordan Valley,
The aerial tramway to the ancient fortress of Masada,
An isolated rock plateau in the Judaean Desert,
The last stand of Jewish patriots against the Roman army,

Where Jews chose death rather than slavery.
Remains of living quarters and bathing areas,
A gift shop cafeteria that gave Shimshon a free lunch.

Suspended in time, we floated in the Dead Sea,
Salty and full of minerals where no fauna nor flora could survive.
We covered each other with mud for a photo op,
Showered and bought a bag of sea salt in the gift shop.
With our impurities and dead skin removed,
We were healthy and invigorated
Driving back to Jerusalem past the Qumran caves
Where the Dead Sea Scrolls were discovered accidentally
By Bedouin teenagers tending their goats.
Large clay jars written on parchment in eleven caves,
More than two thousand years old,
Fragments, parts of every book of the Old Testament
And the earliest version of the Ten Commandments.
I envisioned one of the teenagers
Throwing a rock into a cave, hitting a jar,
And hearing the strange sound of, "Thou shalt not kill."

We took a taxi to The Philadelphia,
An underground Turkish restaurant in the Muslim neighborhood.
As young women smoked aromatic apple tobacco from a hookah,
The proud owner welcomed us with salads, no alcohol,
Chose our halal dinner, roasted lamb shank,
Vegetables, couscous, and fruit.
We were treated as emissaries,
The only foreigners in a room with no controversy.

In the morning, I asked Shimshon how he was doing,
He replied, "Eh," with a palms-up, so-so hand gesture.
We boarded his van and drove north,
Walked around an excavated Roman amphitheater,
A valley of tels, huge mounds of debris from past generations.

We asked to visit the Amit Clubhouse in Upper Nazareth,
A non-profit organization where adults with mental illness
Do the work to get their lives back.
My wife was a volunteer at a clubhouse in Bellevue,
Invited as a guest of honor at Amit,
The first of its kind in Israel,
Over a hundred multi-cultural members,
Jews, Muslims, Christians, Ethiopians all proud of their community.
Some worked across the street at the Elite Candy Factory,
Internationally renowned for Chanukah chocolate coins.
Shimshon talked in several languages with everyone in the room,
Enjoyed the camaraderie and spaghetti.

At the Hamei Tveria hot springs south of Tiberius,
My wife and Shimshon drank black coffee at the snack bar
While I rented a towel and locker to enjoy a thermal bath
Known for its curative powers for more than 3,000 years,
Where Jesus might have cured the sick there,
And Solomon sought demons to heal his kingdom's ailing people
By stoking the fires in the earth below to heat up the water.
In this luxurious spa next to more Roman ruins,
Solomon told me that the water should have been hotter.

An evening sunset in Tiberius on the Sea of Galilee,
Jogging in the morning past the Tomb Mark of the Matriarchs,
Moses' mother, sister, and wife,
Shimshon took us off route to the Golan Heights,
Captured from Syria by Israel during the Six-Day War.
We explored military bunkers,
Oak trees as shelters from aerial bombardment,
A wooden fence with barbed wire at the border,
Rusted tanks half-buried in the sand,
Campaigns to clear the land mines,
Remains of war thirty miles from Damascus.
Shimshon knew the history, lived with the sound of bombardments.

The ruins at Tel Dan Nature Reserve,
Source of the Jordan River with excavations of an ancient city,
The prophets warned about enemy empires
And being carted off to captivity.
We were free to explore little niches in the rock walls,
Rivulets at the base of Mount Hermon,
Peaceful headwaters of the Jordan River.

Shawarma for lunch in Kiryat Shmona,
The Town of Eight named after people who died
In the 1920 Battle of Tel Hai
Between a Shiite Arab Militia and Jewish farmers.
A fast food restaurant in an area under construction,
Serving spit-roasted layers of lamb wrapped in pita,
Topped with lettuce, tomatoes, yogurt and tahini sauces,
Sipping tall glasses of Turkish coffee.
Two IDF young soldiers with Uzi submachine guns
Smiled bashfully as they ordered.

An hour drive to the 16th century city Safed,
Home of kabbalistic mystics, twisted alleyways, and modern art galleries.
Then Haifa, our hotel overlooking the Bahai Gardens on Mount Carmel,
The harbor lit at night like a mirror of the stars,
Our private, mesmerizing pilgrimage on the coast.

The Lebanese border gate seventy-five miles from Beirut,
Guarded by young male and female Israeli soldiers,
The two-minute cable car descending calm and casual
To seventy meters above sea level at a 60-degree angle
To the grottos, white rock walls with flakes of black gneiss,
A source of flint for man's earliest weapons
That protected the cavernous tunnels
Once only accessed by native swimmers and divers.

Caesarea on the Mediterranean,
An ancient Phoenician settlement rebuilt by the Romans,
The excavation of a temple, amphitheater, and hippodrome,
Chariot races for entertainment.
Shimshon's friend at a gift shop,
Gave us discounts on a silver watch and a painted plate.
Driving south, we tried to remember
Everything that we had seen and learned,
As another long, historic day ended in Tel Aviv.

A morning walk in Jaffa, port of the ancient Canaanites,
Ransacked by Napoleon in 1799,
Thousands of Muslim soldiers massacred,
Marched into a vast square and shot.
When all of the cartridges had been spent,
Those remaining were dispatched with bayonets and knives,

A pyramid of dead and dying bodies dripping blood,
More perished later in an epidemic of bubonic plague.
A statue of Napoleon stood in front of the souvenir shop
For tourists to take photo shots.

Travel weary in Tel Aviv, we needed to rest,
Gave Shimshon a day off to visit his sister.
Wearing bathing suits, we drank Turkish coffee
In an outdoor restaurant with beach chairs and small tables on the sand,
Grilled scallops on salad greens, not Kosher,
Waiters finding us among sunbathers.
Now traveling from meal to meal,
That evening a taxi to a popular restaurant,
Young male and female soldiers socializing at tables,
Tavor rifles hanging on the backs of their chairs,
Our waiter took me to a display of different cuts of steak.

We travelled through the Bible,
Thousands of years of history, war and survival,
A land of conflict, religious strife, and torment,
The quest for territory and power,
People at war longing for peace.
I bought a silver *shofar* paperweight
At the airport with my last shekels,
A replica of the Holy City on top,
Shalom in Hebrew.
We hugged Shimshon, could not let go,
Like saying goodbye to a brother
We would never see again.
He had opened up his life for us,

Put Israel into ours,
And sent us on our way to the gate.
We had someplace else to go,
Passports in hand.
Shimshon had his home,
His family, and everyone in Israel.

On the plane we looked out the window,
Could imagine Shimshon driving his van,
Waving to his friends,
Eating dinner with his wife,
And drinking tea.
We printed photos at home,
Put them in frames and albums,
A small part of our lives
Measured in miles and miles of Israel.
We did not go to the West Bank or the Gaza border,
But we are there now, every day
In the news and on television,
Praying for peace and human dignity,
A two-state solution for Israelis and Palestinians.
Ten days cannot capture millennia,
But like the Ten Commandments,
Ten days can shed some light
On the principles of Judaism, Christianity, and Islam,
All the people on earth who should care about each other,
Coexist safely, share their cultures, beliefs, and values,
And always have someplace they can go to live their lives.

On the Other Side

Ghosts come to life,
Talk out loud,
Souls make sense.
They are the brides
Joined by grooms,
Parents joined by children,
Children joined by parents,
Husbands and their wives,
Looking exactly like when they were alive,
Shirts with no stains,
Suits with no wrinkles,
Skin with no blemishes,
Every song in the afterlife.

The food tastes good,
Perfectly cooked,
Not health food or healthy food,
Just food food.
Nothing matters,
Around the margins,
Disease free,
Smiles handshakes and hugs,
Every color and hairstyle,
All languages understood.

Many wonder that this is all in vain,
Thoughts of what could be,

Knowing what was and is,
Hearing and seeing,
Being a being,
Fearing and believing,
Comforted by hopes,
Prayers for what they do not know,
Like water that does not evaporate,
Days without nights,
Pleasure without pain.

I walk among them all about,
Listen to their words and dreams,
Let their thoughts dissipate
Without worry or surmise.
I live in the world they live in,
But clearly in a different world,
Gospel overlayed with science,
Which leads astray defiance,
And weary doomsday reliance.
I would pity them if it mattered,
Their beliefs obliterated and shattered,
But I smile and let them be,
For maybe I will see them,
No longer doubt,
And welcome their angels,
Good heavens!
When I step out.

Epilogue

> "... approach thy grave, like one who wraps the drapery of his couch about him, and lies down to pleasant dreams."
> — William Cullen Bryant, "Thanatopsis"

I write my will over and over,
Every day a new way to leave behind
All that I am apparently worth,
Memorabilia, victories and defeats,
As I limp, grunt, and gasp with old age,
Unfilled prescriptions, unfulfilled aspirations.

My attorney charges a fee to prepare it succinctly
Into an immortal estate binder,
Like an embalmed body in a vinyl coffin,
With legal language that avoids probate,
Hereafter instructions that will rise from the tomb
To bloom silently cold in the great unknown moonlight.

The pen I use to sign this final directive,
Almost out of ink like a last breath,
Attempts to spell a semblance of meaning.
No more codicils to notarize,
This testament tries to die honestly
Without fanfare, living in trust.

Executing this instrument on the near side of death,
I appear to be of sound mind and memory,
Not acting under duress, menace, fraud,
Undue influence, misrepresentation, or frivolity.

Just give me a clean exit, let me rest alone in peace,
Distribute all my property, extinguish all the paperwork,
Everything bequeathed to my beneficiaries,
So that they can write their wills with less than solemn ceremony,
Again and again and again,
And look forward to sharing the inevitable destination
And ultimate resolution of life.

Ship in a Bottle

Look at the sailors,
Suspended in time,
Restrained by a cork,
Not breathing from port to starboard.

Some have gone to war,
Others on holiday,
Voyages around the world,
Buried at the bottom of the ocean.

All hands on deck fore and aft,
Standing on a whittled piece of wood,
Awaiting firm orders from stem to stern,
The paralyzed hull above a sea of blue putty.

The bowsprit holds the rigging,
For toothpick masts and booms,
Connected deftly across the beam,
With hinges and thread to raise the sails.

I live in my tinted bottle,
Try to stay even keeled,
Asleep at night packed flat,
Awake In the morning, a sharp tweezer spars me.

Sets me on the open seas,
Puts me at the helm,
To turn my weathered wheel,
And navigate the relentless rudder.

Captive to the gusty winds of change,
Plotting my course with dying stars,
A captain whose sails are loosely trimmed,
I will only go so far.

Sunken Ships

In the bottom of my ocean
Lies a treasure
That phantom divers
Try to find.

With elusive underwater gear,
And without fear,
They supply oxygen
To what is hidden
Deep in the cold environs
Of my silence.

What they find is still alive,
With shallow breaths
And even greater depth,
Recalling imaginary pleasures,
And chanting a chorus
Of reminiscent dreams.

Below the surface
Light shines,
Illuminates the secrets
That have never been shared
And never will,
Destinies of dreary evenings,
Uninspired thoughts that have lost their way

And disappeared into darkness
That will never see another day.

The salvage operation is costly,
Recovering the cargo in a frigid sea
Requires sleepless nights
And restless waves and currents,
The shipwreck more survivor than casualty,
No guarantee of destiny,
No eternal infinity set completely free.

Aphrodite, *Alcaic* stanzas

She buys rainbow microgreens at Stater Bros,
Organizes linens, plastic storage bins,
Drinks red, white alcohol-removed wine,
Writes Vote Forward letters for Democracy.

Prednisone calms artery inflammation,
Insomnia manages to take the night,
Hephaestus grills Chilean sea bass,
They imbibe purified water on ice.

The past portends future with impunity,
Her smiles and laughter empower unity,
In every moment, vacation,
Paradise ensconced in celebration.

Waiting in ER

Waiting is not an emergency
It's worse
Just call the hearse
And hope it's not stuck in traffic
Don't panic
Your time will come soon enough
Pack up your stuff
Sit in a chair
Don't breathe the stale air

There's a baby crying
An old man dying
And a cash only vending machine
With nothing healthy
If that's what you're trying

Hour after hour
Until your name is finally called
Remember your date of birth
Older or younger than some
Vitals better or worse than others
Go home and die if you had your druthers

Now you have to pass some tests
List all your medications
Out of the country vacations

When you last took ibuprofen
As you become a human pin cushion
Drawing blood in painful fashion
Nurses check if your heart is beating
And that you've been regular and eating

You drive to urgent care all your life
Now elevated to a much higher level
Biopsies under the knife
To check your veins and arteries
Lying on a bed horizontally
Trying to win life's lottery
On the operating table
Despite your diet of green leafy vegetables

You know the routine
Memorized the drill
Just take one more pill
An IV drip
Don't make a scene
On your last trip
You've got nothing more to lose
This isn't a Viking Cruise

The wait is over
You made it baby
Everyone is proud of you
You should be too

Another First Seder

> "Why is this night different from all the other nights?"
> — *A Passover Haggadah*

I saved a shank bone
From a dinner last year,
Wrapped in aluminum foil,
In the freezer,
Not much of a sacrifice,
Just sitting on a shelf in the door,
In frozen silence,
Like the rest of us.

It's a good question if this night is any different.
It might as well be.
I'm roasting a leg of lamb,
Not a brisket,
Bought the second to last
Box of kosher-for-Passover matzah,
Couldn't find macaroons,
Serving Halvah from Turkey instead,
Not friendly toward Israel,
Found a recipe for Persian charoset,
Also not friendly,
Apple, banana, dates, and cashews.
We will still celebrate the fruit of the vine,
With Kedem grape juice not Manischewitz wine,

Practice good deeds and thank life,
With imported Yehuda original gefilte fish,
Hard boiled eggs,
One shell burnt,
A symbol of mourning.

I did not need to be freed from Egypt,
Never even been there.
My exodus from Manhattan long ago,
More than forty years,
Ended up in Palm Desert,
A paradise like a promised land
An oasis in blue sky Coachella Valley,
One could not ask for more,
Lots of sun, wind, and sand.

My travels took me to Jerusalem,
Walked all four quarters of the Holy City,
Ate lamb with couscous at a Muslim restaurant,
Listened to the morning call to prayer.
Now I can barely watch the evening news,
The horrors in Gaza,
What little left of life is like over there.
Where are the mitzvot,
Freedom for all people,
Commandments and good deeds,
Freedom from burdens?

We sit around the Passover table,
Follow traditions in a more modern way,

Enjoy the meal,
Sober and somber,
Wondering about whom to praise,
Or how many glasses of juice to raise,
Asking more than four questions,
Not knowing the answers,
And searching for a promise,
Like a hidden piece of matzoh,
That the children can never find without clues,
Like people in exile suffering a life they did not choose,
As Dylan sang, "When you got nothing, you got nothing to lose."
Except the hope for freedom,
The termination of injustice,
And peace for everyone,
For all people.

We can't just wait for next year,
We have to persist, resist, and persevere,
It has to be right now, this minute, this moment,
Today is even too late.
Hear the cry,
The world has suffered too many plagues.
Open the door for Elijah and turn the key,
Pave every single path with hope,
Separate the matzahs into thirds,
And end every seder with these four simple words.
"May all be free."

Boulder Drop

One mile west of Index,
The ice-cold waters of the Skykomish
Rushed fiercely toward Puget Sound,
My spirit protected by a wet suit,
Running rapids in a rubber ducky,
With double blades and trepidation.

A Canadian rodeo champion thought it fun,
After filming waterfalls
For television commercials,
Hiking through the forest,
Lugging kayaks and camera gear.

My son up for adventure,
Persuaded me to join along,
Wear a helmet, step into the river,
Paddle with the current,
Turbulent waves reflecting the sun.

I agreed not to portage
This Class IV rapid,
Not knowing any better,
And trying to be a good dad,
Supportive of youthful impulse.

The guide said if you dump,
Keep your feet up
To not get caught in the rocks.
This was the first sign
That I was way over my head.

I came out of my boat on the first drop,
Held my breath as long as I could,
All I saw were bubbles,
Like in a washing machine,
Trying to keep my feet up.

I popped up two or three times,
Gasped for air,
And then it was over,
Washed into an eddy,
Clinging to the rocks.

Some parents do anything for their children.
I was one of them,
Time and time again,
This time putting my life on the line,
Hoping that everything would be fine.

In Peace Rest

He always gave to homeless on the street,
Each turn in life a new anomaly.
At golf for every shot he would compete,
Grinned on whiffs, "You've got to be kidding me."
A nerve sheath tumor did not set him back,
Skiing, tennis, wrestling, an ethnic dish,
The Marine Crucible, guitar soundtrack,
Loved to fish even if he caught no fish.
He befriended those with daily struggles,
Wanted to live in the woods, his castle,
Raise chickens and goats, grow some vegetables,
Away from people and all the hassle.
His unpredictable life now at ease,
With great memories, forever at peace.

The Last Sunday in Sacramento

Aaron Dana Lyon
February 7, 1980 – October 27, 2024

A cold Sapporo
Washes down the taste of loss
Peace at Sushi Hook

About the Author

I was born yesterday in Palm Desert.
I watered the lantana, tried to write a poem.
Metamucil is my favorite cocktail,
needing to ingest forty grams of fiber daily.
Today, I called my bank to establish a pay on death card.
Tomorrow, I will say my last words.

Kenneth Lyon was born in Manhattan, New York City, in 1947. He graduated from Clarkson University with a Bachelor of Science in Mathematics, The Johns Hopkins University Writing Seminars with a Master of Arts in Creative Writing Poetry, and the University of Denver with a PhD in Creative Writing Fiction. Dr. Lyon was an educator for forty-five years, teaching at all levels first grade through college in Maryland, Vermont, Colorado, The People's Republic of China, and Washington State. He was also a school principal, a central office administrator, a Hearing Officer, and a Harassment, Intimidation, and Bullying Compliance Officer. After he retired, Dr. Lyon continued his anti-bullying work as a ventriloquist for five years, presenting at schools, clubs, various organizations, and the International Ventriloquist Society. Dr. Lyon lives with his wife and dog in Palm Desert, California, and is a member of Desert Poets.

Acknowledgments

Thank you to all who have read my poems. I write and share new poems with Desert Poets in Sun City Palm Desert, and their constructive criticism has been invaluable. The ten of us write to different prompts suggested for each meeting. These "dreaded prompts" get me thinking creatively away from my favorite themes. I also share poems with Sun City Writers Circle—novelists, playwrights, and non-fiction authors who meet monthly. I am fortunate to belong to these two communities. Many poems that I shared with them have found their way to publication.

When my wife and I have someone to our house for dinner, I often read a poem and watch their reaction. That is extremely helpful. I have also recently recited poems for a few people who never read poetry, and now they are fans of my work. I always appreciate it when someone reads one of my poems and relates it to their own life. I have sold several books at arts and crafts fairs and have received a lot of positive feedback. While writing is a solitary endeavor, I grow by connecting with my audience.

Robert McDowell continues to be a wonderful editor and publisher. His direct comments are very meaningful, especially when he says things like, "You must change the last line. It's not good, and it sabotages the poem. Please repair that." He is always right. I would also like to thank Ray Rhamey, who designed all parts of this book, from front to back covers, and everything in between. His publishing vision and expertise brought this book to life.

I wouldn't be a poet today without Roberta's support, encouragement, and love. She reads and edits my poems, listens to my poetic and not-so-poetic ramblings, and puts up with me writing in the middle of the night with ideas that surface in my sleep.

The world near me and around me also play their part, for better and worse. I see and hear things that inspire me to react. Life is boundless, and I try to push the limits as much as possible. *Pushing the Limits* is that boundless push.

ntent.com/pod-product-compliance
LLC

'660